FIRST
GUITAR
CHORDS

Cover design by Pearce Marchbank, Studio Twenty
Cover photography by George Taylor
Compiled and arranged by Arthur Dick
Computer management by Adam Hay Editorial Design
Music processed by The Pitts

Order No. AM 954173
International Standard Book Number: 0.7119.7222.2

Exclusive Distributors:
Music Sales Corporation
257 Park Avenue South, New York, NY 10010 USA
Music Sales Limited
8/9 Frith Street, London W1V 5TZ England
Music Sales Pty. Limited
120 Rothschild Avenue, Rosebery, Sydney, NSW 2018, Australia

Printed in the United States of America by
Vicks Lithograph and Printing Corporation

Wise Publications
London/New York/Paris/Sydney/Copenhagen/Madrid

CD Track Listing

Track 1 – Tuning Tones
Key of C
Track 2 – C, C6, Cmaj7
Track 3 – Csus4, Dm, Dm7
Track 4 – Em7, F, G7
Track 5 – G9, Am, Bdim
Key of D
Track 6 – D, D6, Dmaj7
Track 7 – Dsus4, Em, Em7
Track 8 – F♯m, G, A7
Track 9 – A9, Bm, C♯dim
Key of E♭
Track 10 – E♭, E♭6, E♭maj7
Track 11 – E♭sus4, Fm, Fm7
Track 12 – Gm, A♭, B♭7
Track 13 – B♭9, Cm, Ddim
Key of E
Track 14 – E, E6, Emaj7
Track 15 – Esus4, F♯m, F♯m7
Track 16 – G♯m, A, B7
Track 17 – B9, C♯m, D♯dim
Key of F
Track 18 – F, F6, Fmaj7
Track 19 – Fsus4, Gm, Gm7
Track 20 – Am, B♭, C7
Track 21 – C9, Dm, Edim
Key of G (Barré)
Track 22 – G, G6, Gmaj7
Track 23 – Gsus4, Am, Am7
Track 24 – Bm7, C, D7
Track 25 – D9, Em, F♯dim
Open G Chords
Track 26 – G, G6, Gmaj7
Track 27 – Gsus4, G7, G7sus4
Track 28 – G9, G6/9, G11
Key of A
Track 29 – A, A6, Amaj7
Track 30 – Asus4, Bm, Bm7
Track 31 – C♯m, D, E7
Track 32 – E9, F♯m7, G♯dim
Key of B♭
Track 33 – B♭, B♭6, B♭maj7
Track 34 – B♭sus4, Cm, Cm7
Track 35 – Dm, E♭, F7
Track 36 – F9, Gm, Adim

First Chords For Guitar provides a pictorial introduction to chord construction. Simply locate the notes on the guitar fretboard by using the chord diagram and then look at the photograph to check the fingering and hand position.

The keys that are included in this book are the most common and provide a useful and comprehensive selection of chord types and voicings. For a further study of keys and chord types please refer to The Complete Guitar Player CD Chord Encyclopædia (AM 90134) available from Music Sales.

Reading Chord Boxes

Chord boxes are diagrams of the guitar neck viewed head upwards, face on as illustrated. The thick horizontal line at the top is the nut, the other horizontal lines are the frets. The vertical lines are the strings starting from E (or 6th) on the left to E (or 1st) on the right.

The black dots indicate where the fingers are placed.

Strings marked with an O are open strings.

Strings marked with an X must not be played.

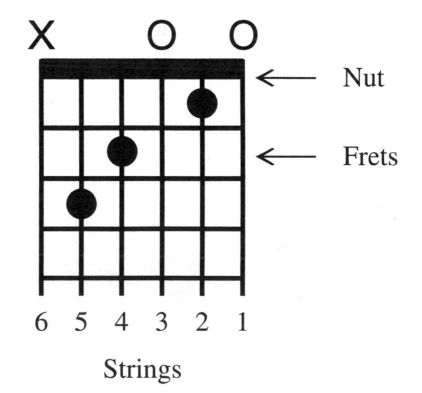

Accurate tuning of the guitar is essential.

The guitar can be tuned with the aid of pitch pipes or dedicated electronic guitar tuners which are available through your local music dealer.

If you do not have a tuning device, you can use relative tuning.

Relative Tuning

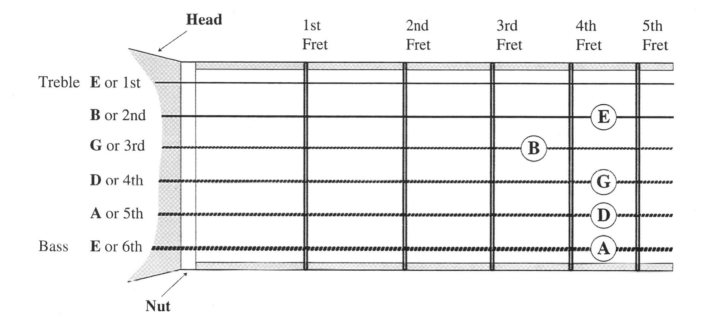

Press down where indicated, one at a time, following the instructions below.

Estimate the pitch of the 6th string as near as possible to E or at least a comfortable pitch (not too high, as you might break other strings in tuning up).

Then, while checking the various positions on the above diagram, place a finger from your left hand on:

the 5th fret of the E or 6th string and **tune the open A** (or 5th string) to the note (A)

the 5th fret of the A or 5th string and **tune the open D** (or 4th string) to the note (D)

the 5th fret of the D or 4th string and **tune the open G** (or 3rd string) to the note (G)

the 4th fret of the G or 3rd string and **tune the open B** (or 2nd string) to the note (B)

the 5th fret of the B or 2nd string and **tune the open E** (or 1st string) to the note (E)

Key of C

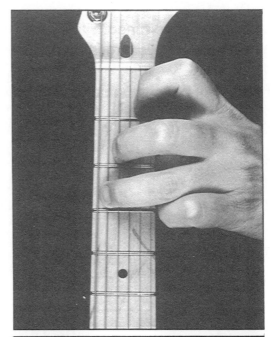

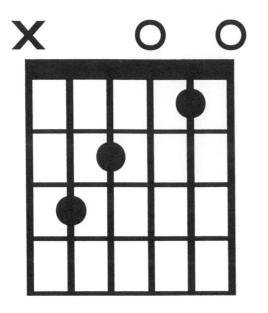

C

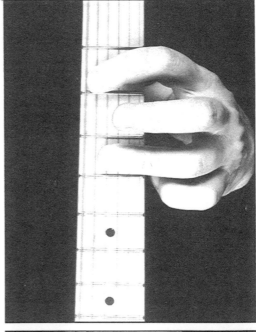

3rd fret

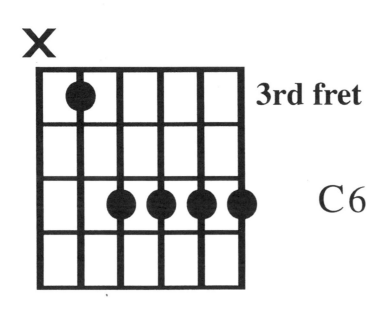

C 6

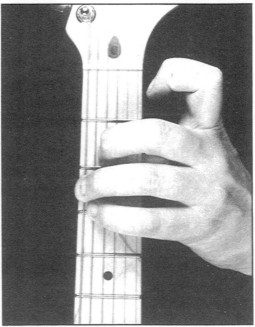

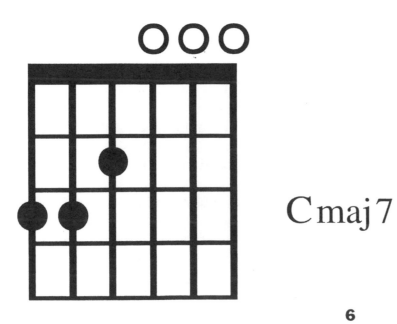

C maj 7

Key of C

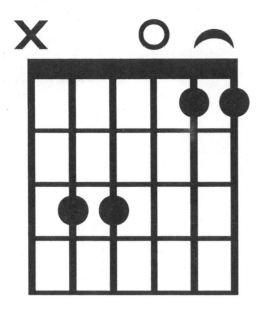

Csus4

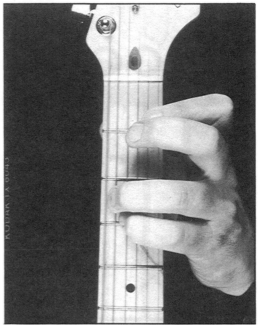

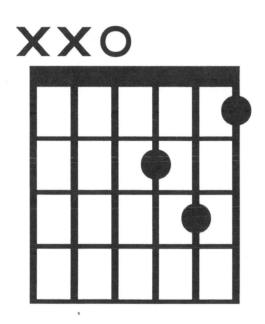

Dm

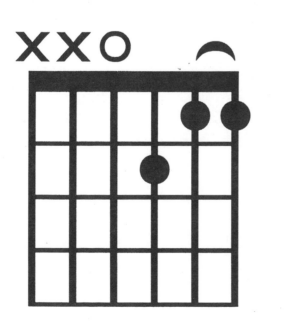

Dm7

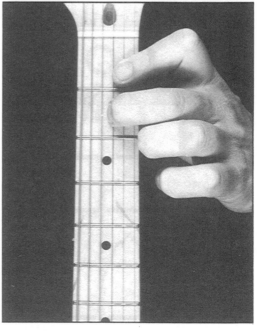

Key of C

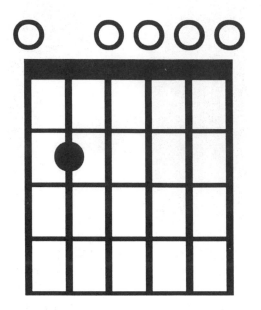

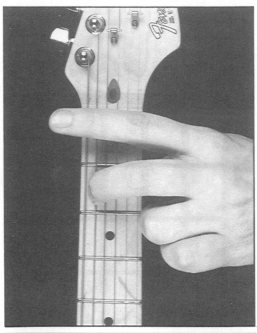

Em7

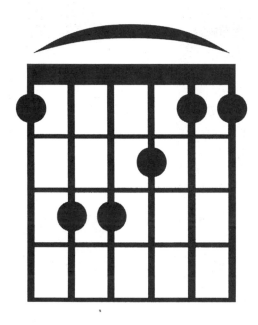

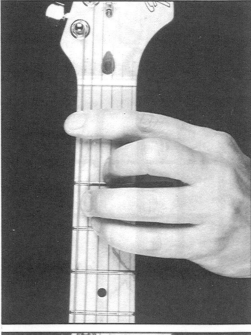

F

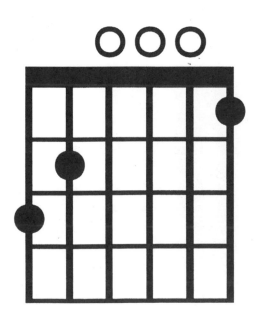

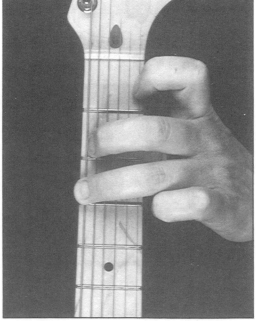

G7

Key of C

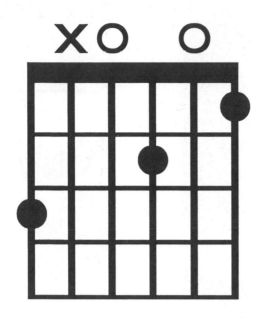

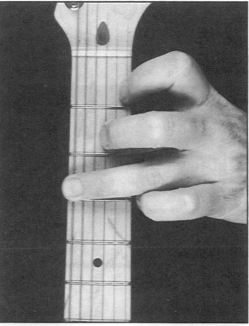

G9

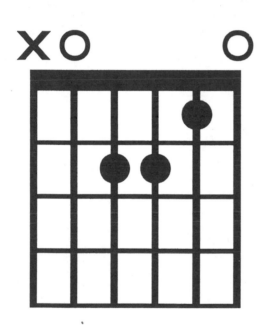

Am

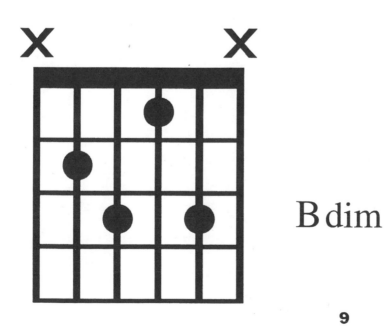

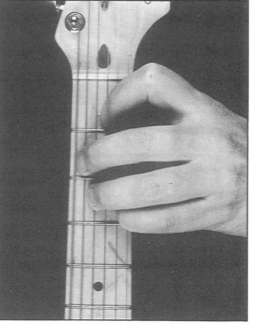

B dim

Key of D

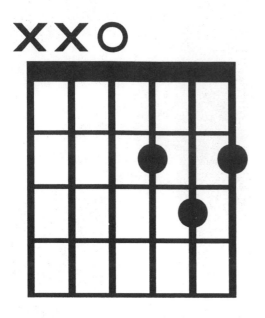

D

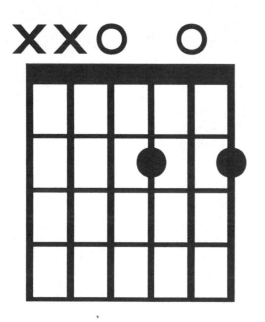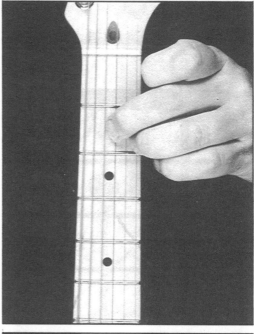

D6

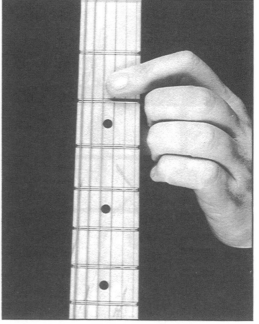

Dmaj7

Key of D

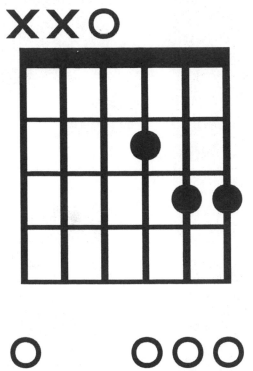

Dsus4

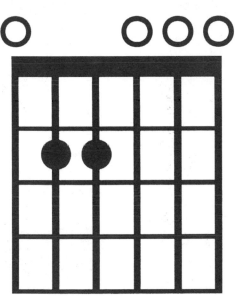

Em

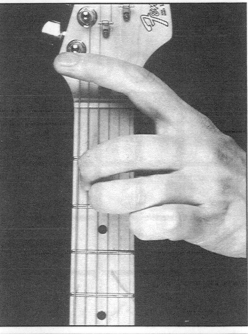

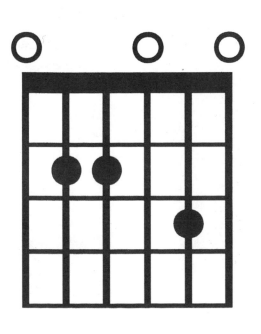

Em7

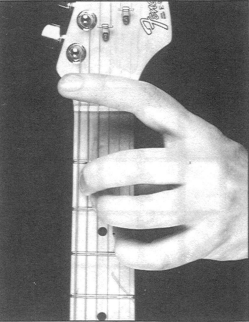

Key of D

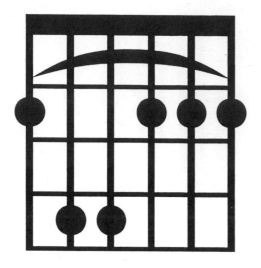

F#m

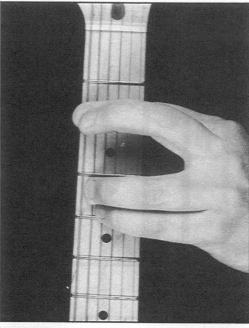

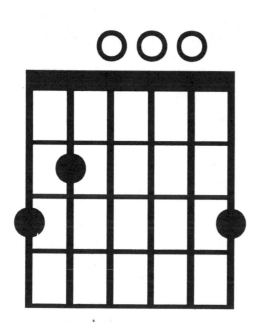

G

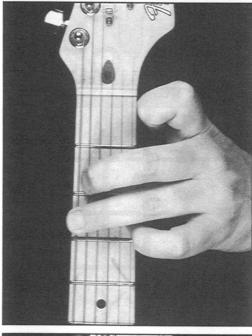

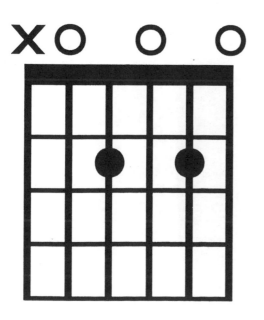

A7

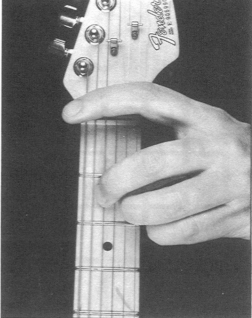

Key of D

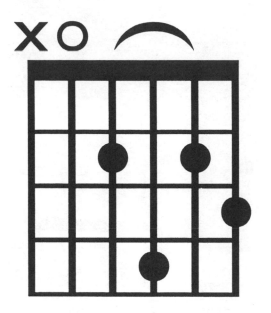

A9

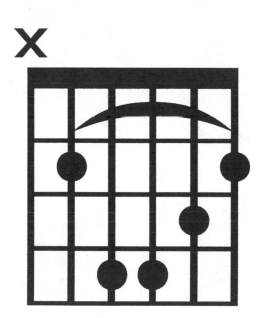

Bm

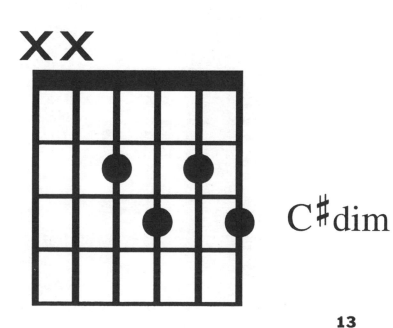

C#dim

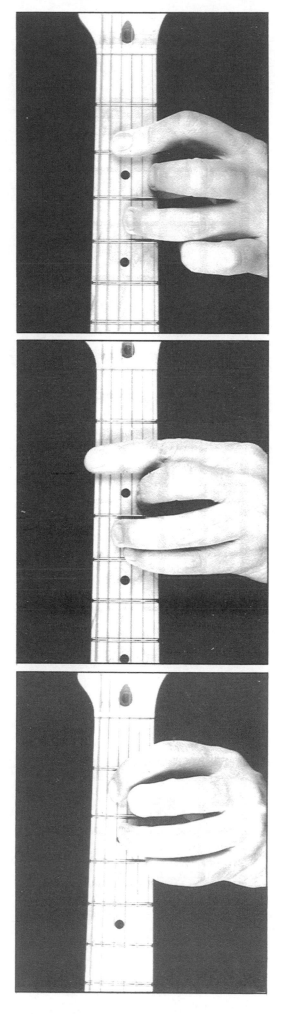

Key of E♭

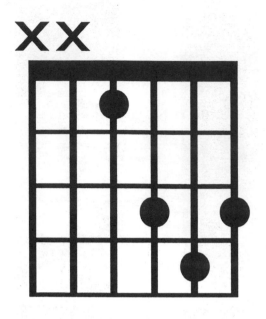

E♭

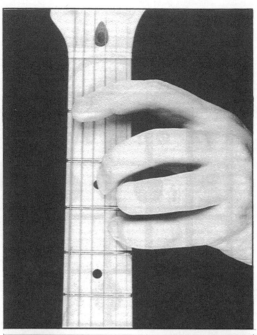

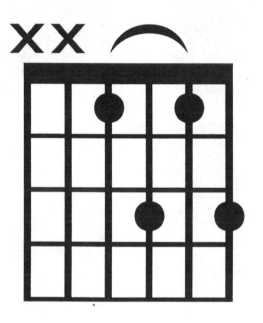

E♭6

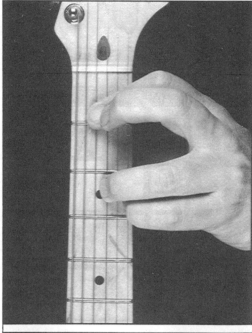

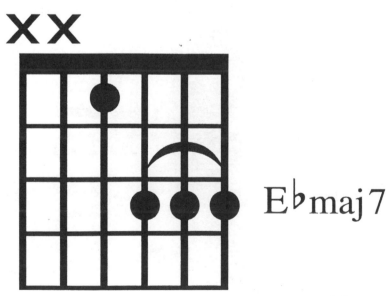

E♭maj7

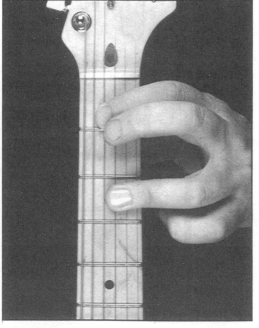

Key of E♭

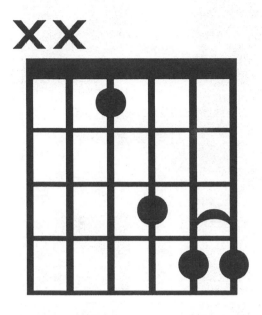

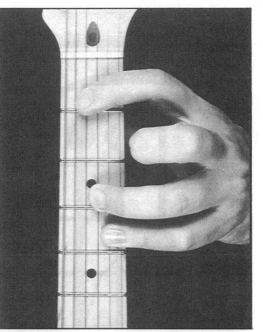

E♭sus4

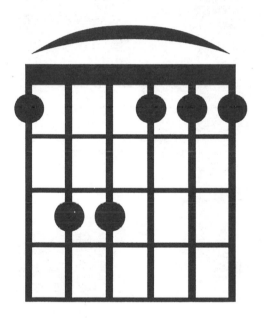

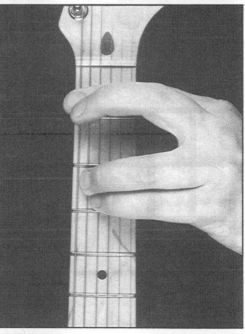

Fm

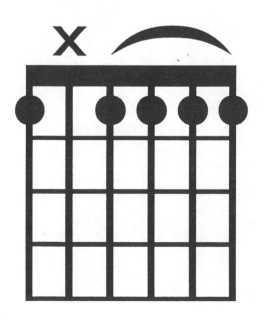

Fm7

Key of E♭

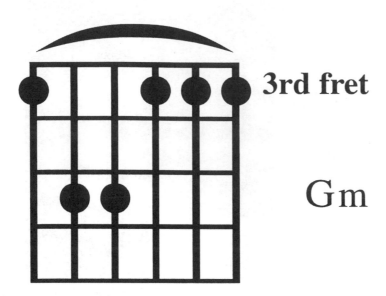

3rd fret

Gm

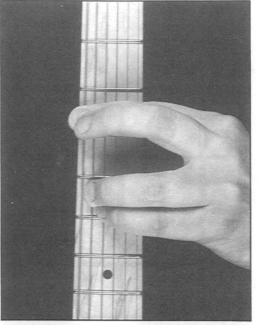

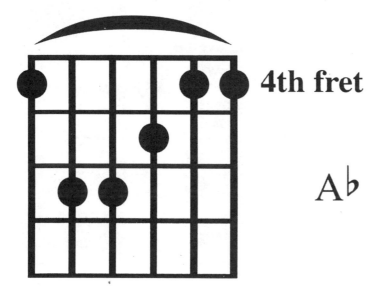

4th fret

A♭

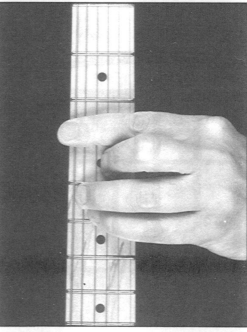

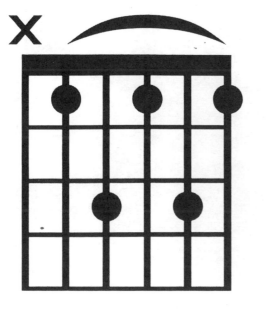

X

B♭7

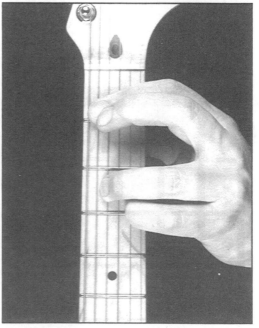

Key of E♭

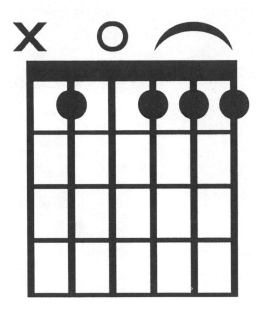

B♭9

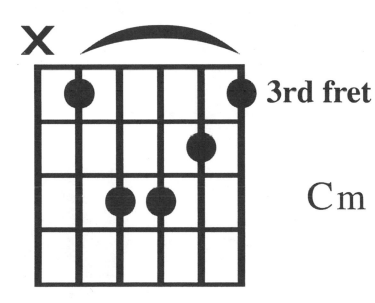

3rd fret

Cm

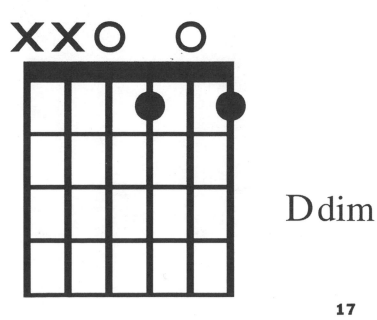

D dim

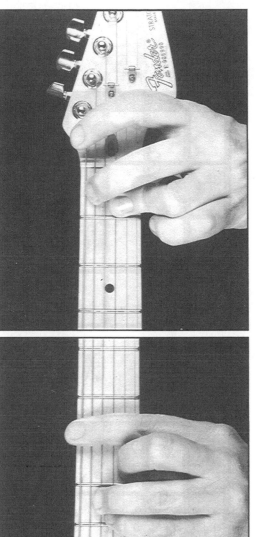

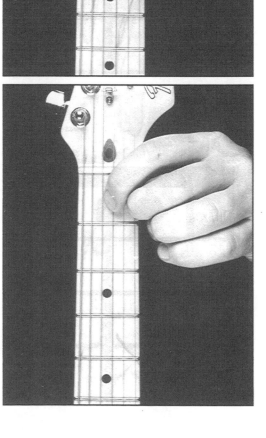

Key of E

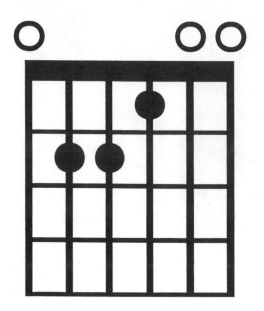

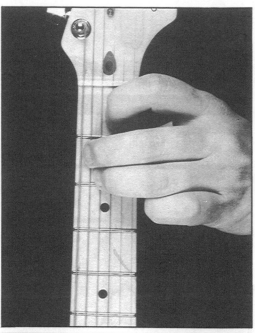

E

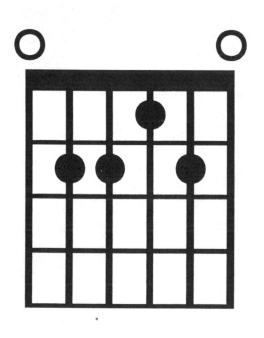

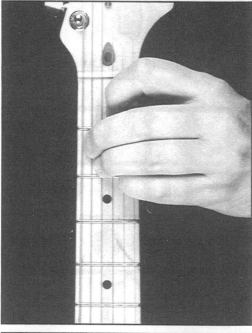

E6

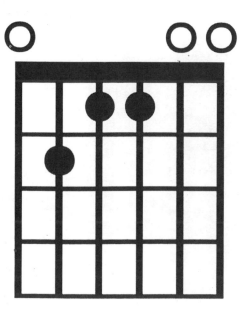

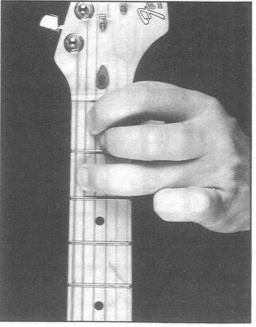

Emaj7

Key of E

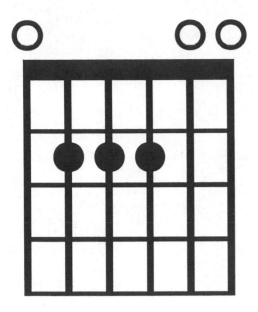

E sus 4

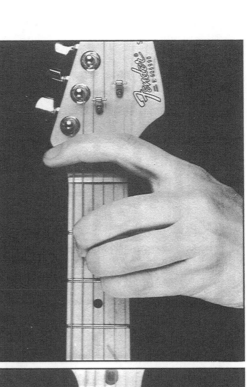

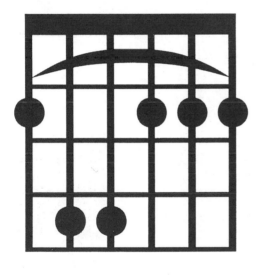

F#m

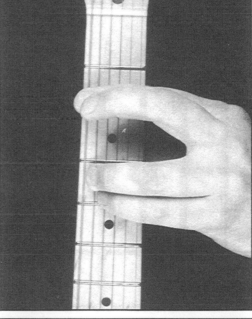

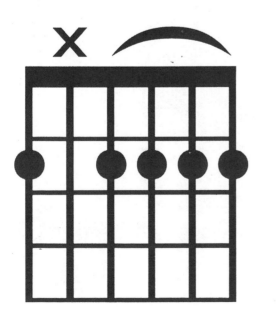

F#m7

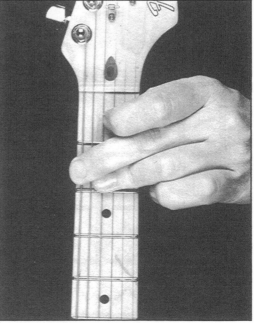

Key of E

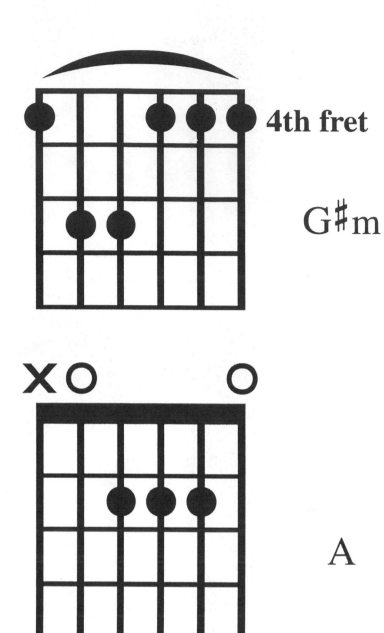

4th fret

G♯m

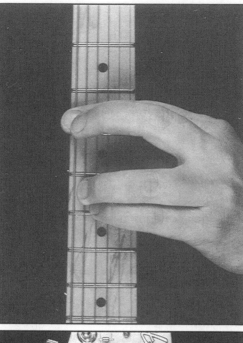

A

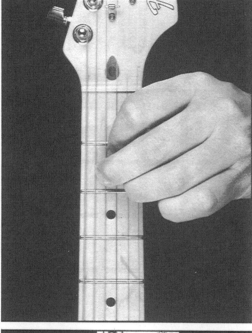

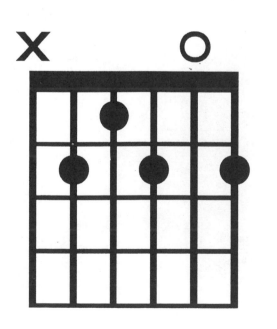

B 7

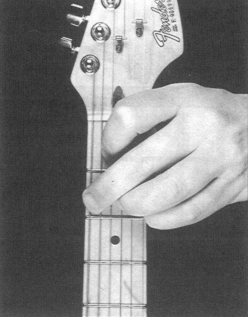

20

Key of E

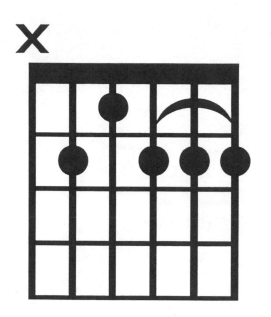

B 9

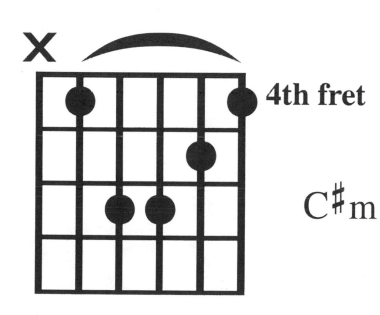

4th fret

C#m

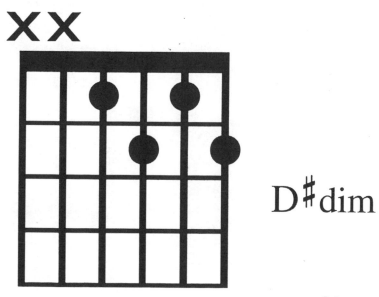

D#dim

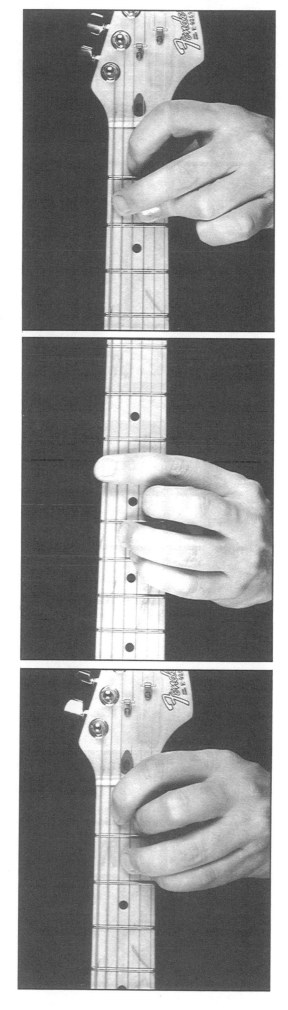

21

Key of F

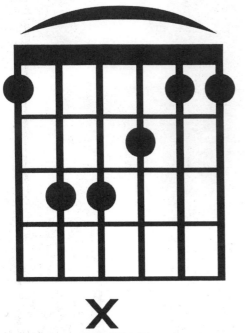

F

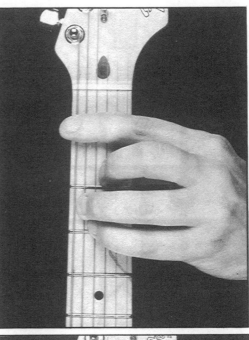

F6

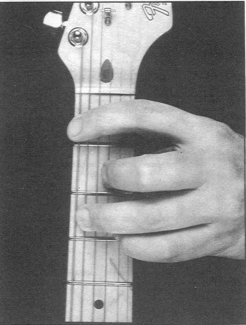

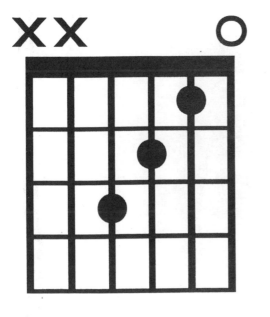

Fmaj7

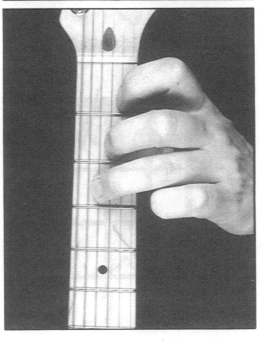

Key of F

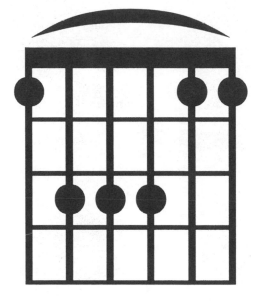

Fsus4

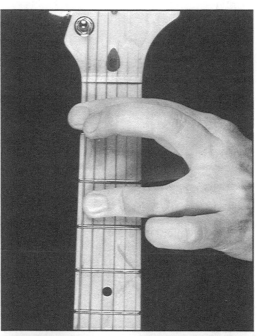

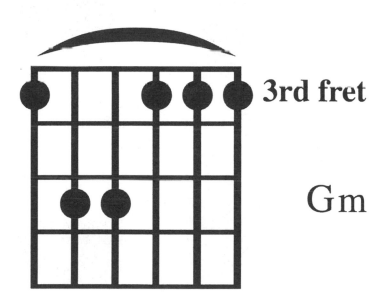

3rd fret

Gm

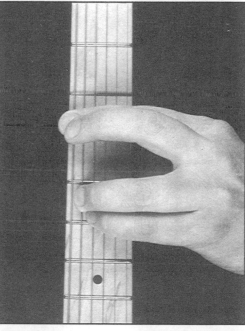

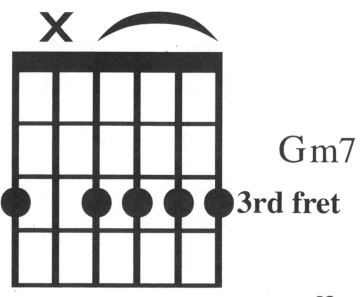

Gm7

3rd fret

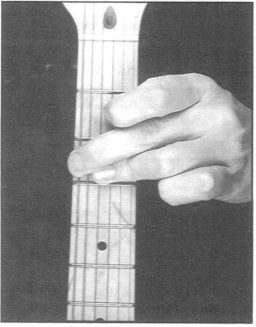

23

Key of F

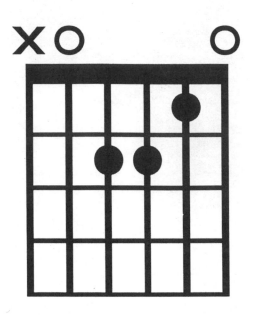

Am

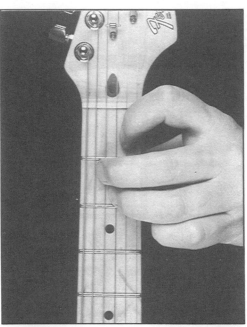

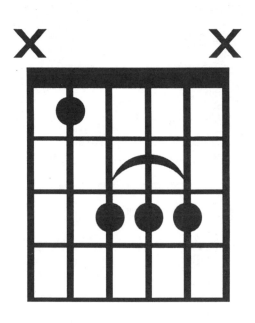

B♭

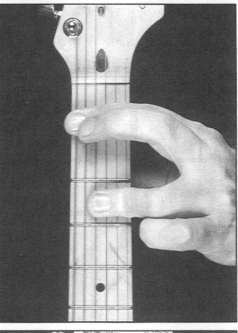

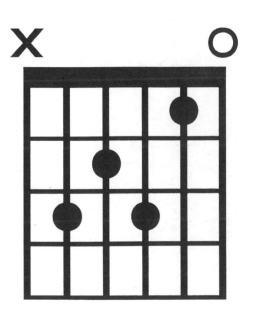

C7

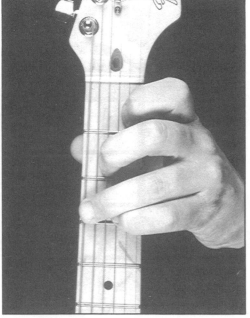

Key of F

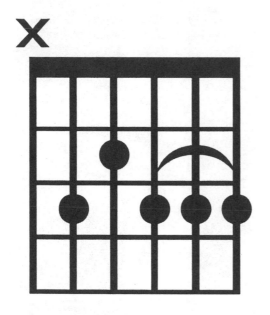

C9

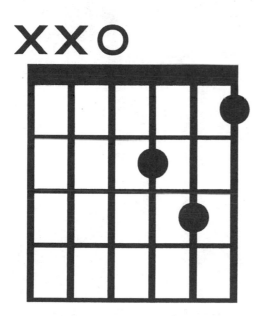

Dm

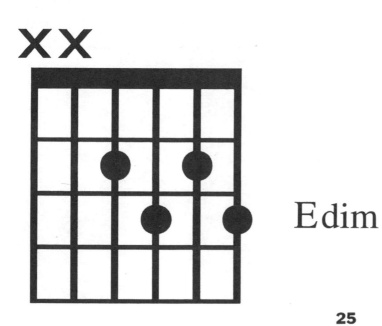

Edim

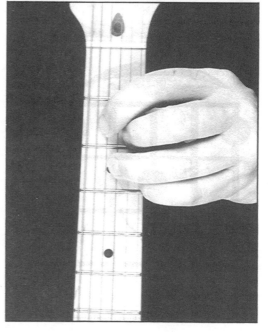

Key of G
(Barré)

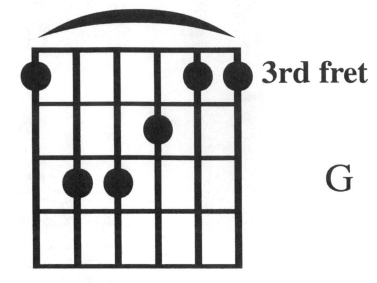

3rd fret

G

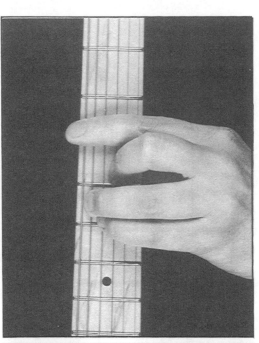

3rd fret

G6

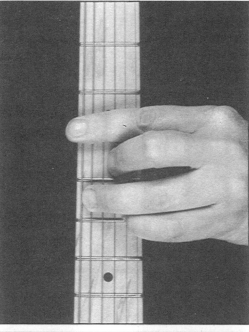

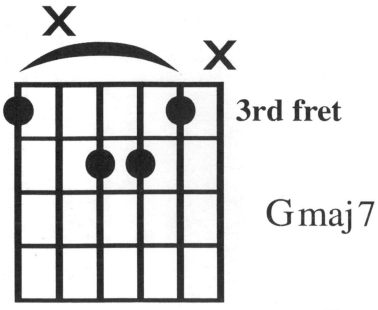

3rd fret

Gmaj7

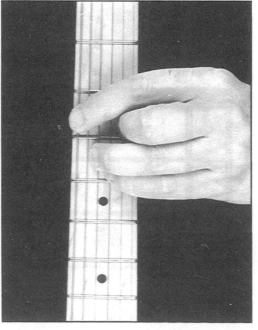

Key of G
(Barré)

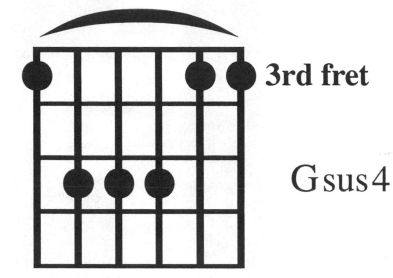

3rd fret

G sus 4

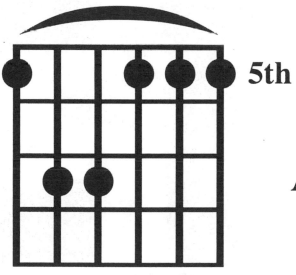

5th fret

Am

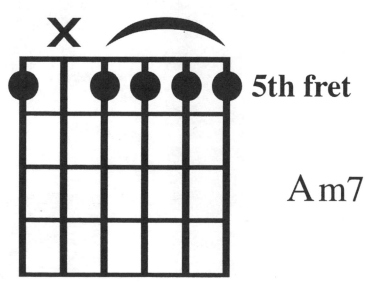

5th fret

Am7

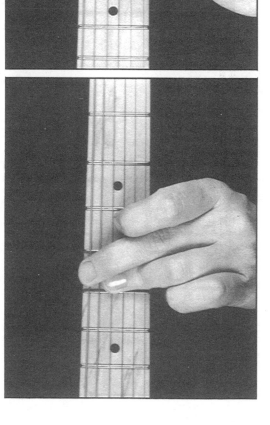

Key of G
(Barré)

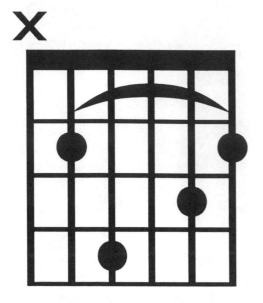

B m7

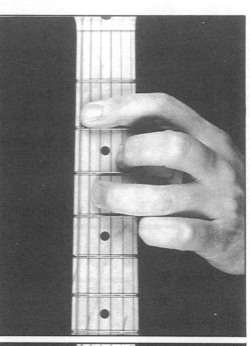

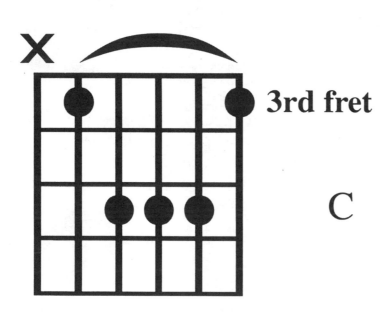

3rd fret

C

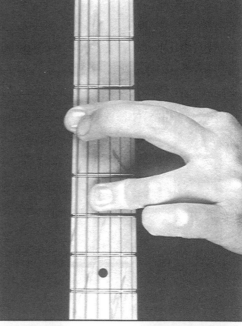

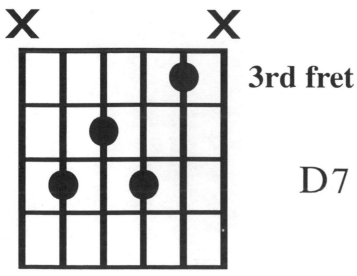

3rd fret

D 7

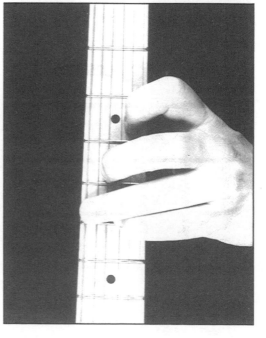

Key of G
(Barré)

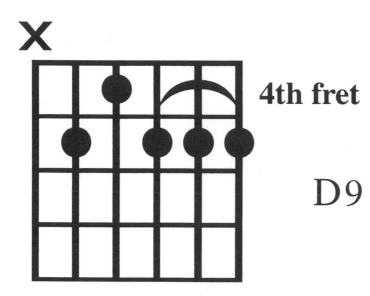

4th fret

D9

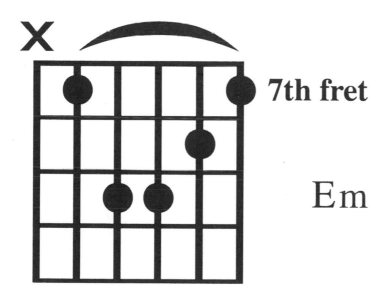

7th fret

Em

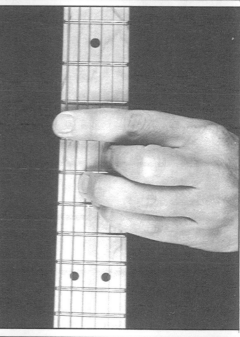

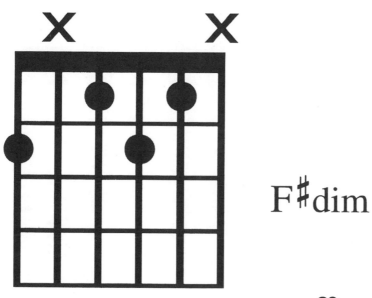

F#dim

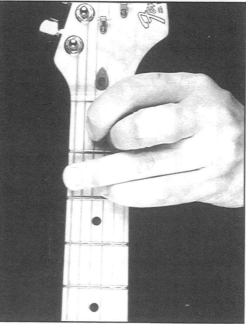

Open G
Chords

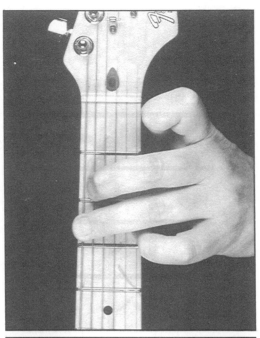

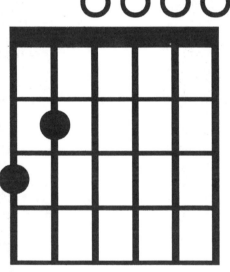

G

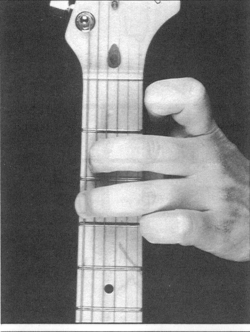

G6

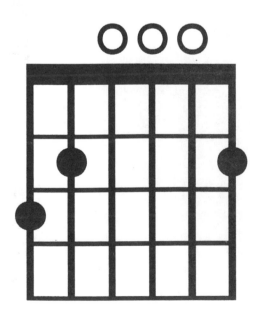

Gmaj7

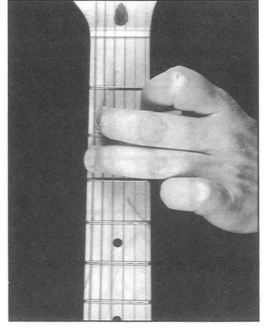

Open G Chords

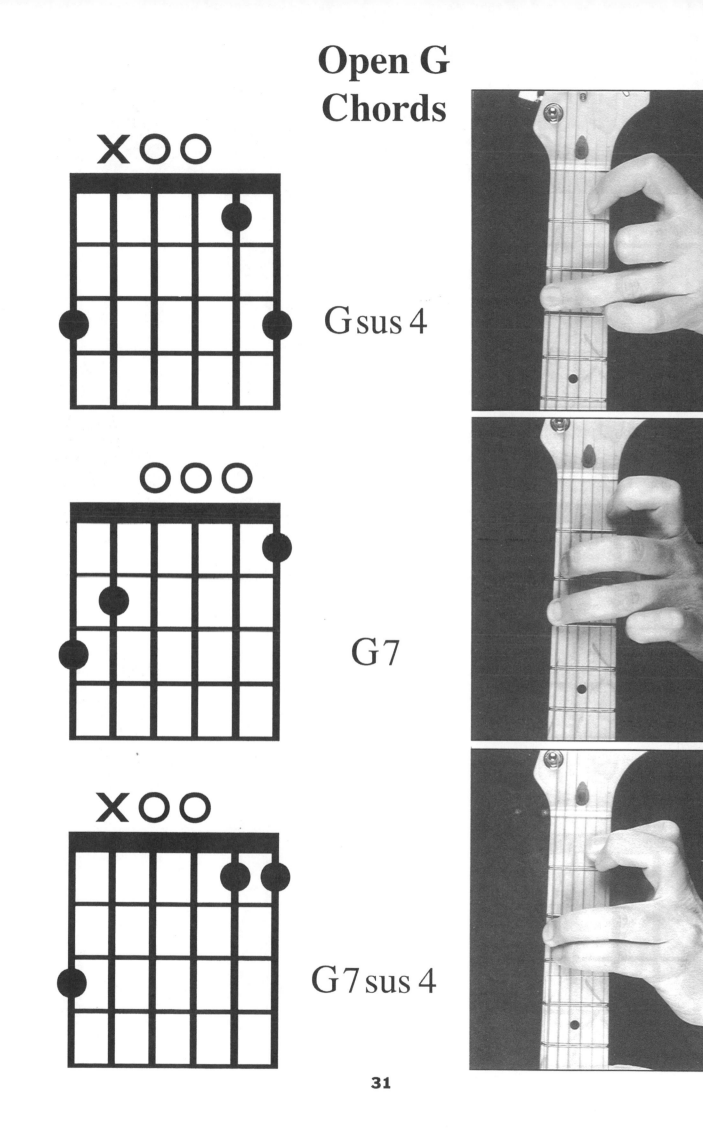

G sus 4

G 7

G 7 sus 4

31

Open G Chords

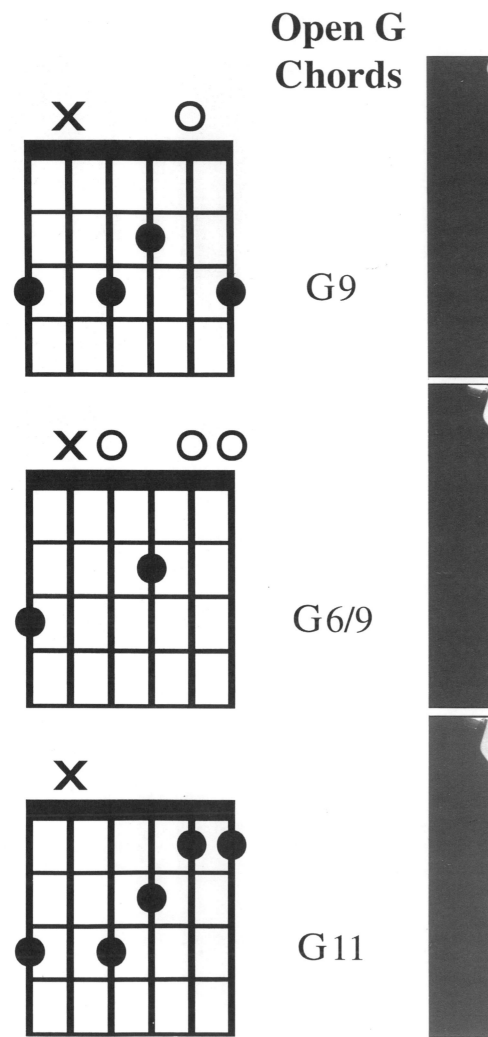

G9

G6/9

G11

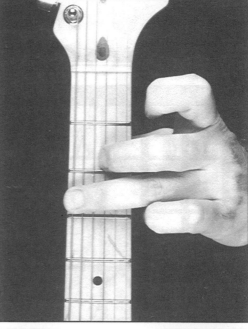

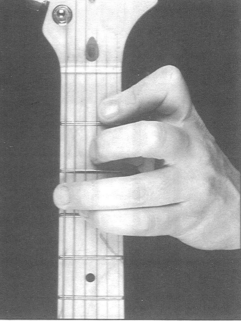

Key of A

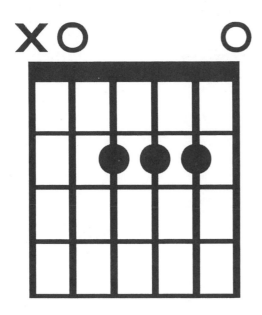

A

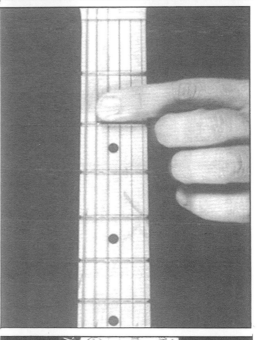

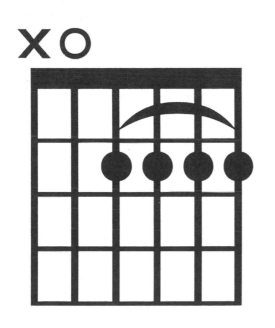

A6

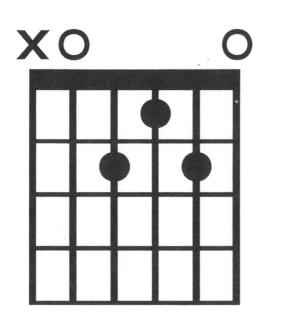

Amaj7

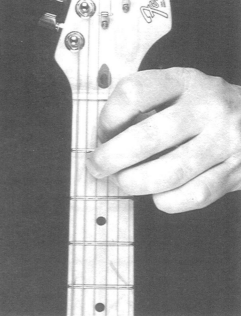

Key of A

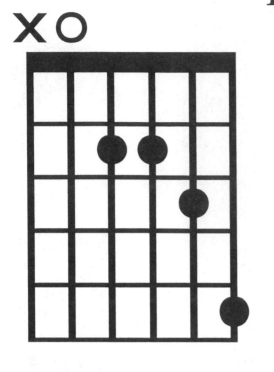

A sus 4

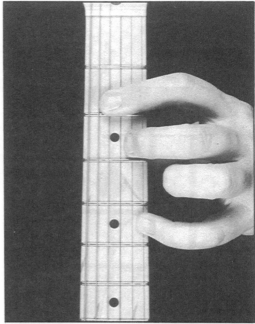

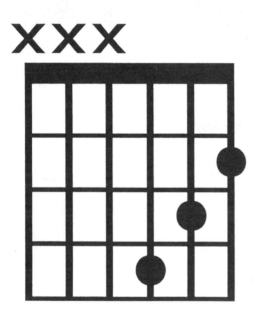

B m

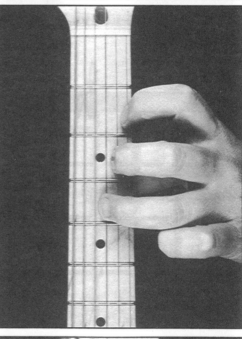

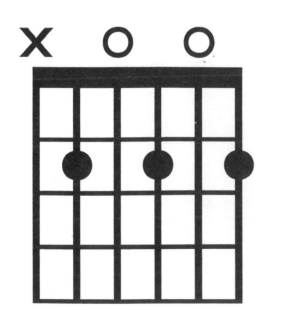

B m 7

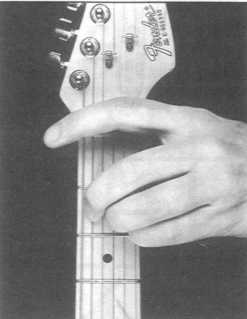

Key of A

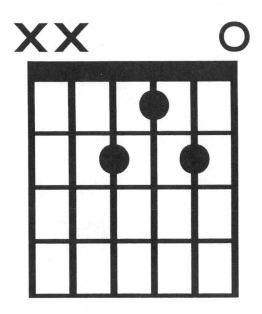

C#m

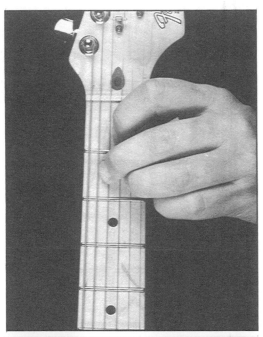

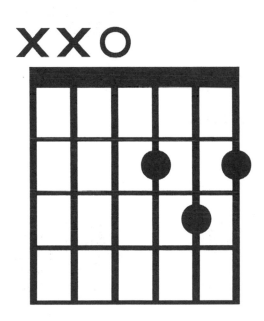

D

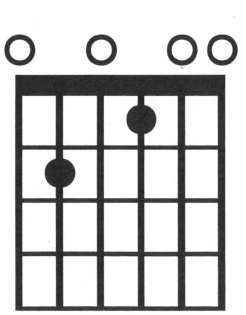

E 7

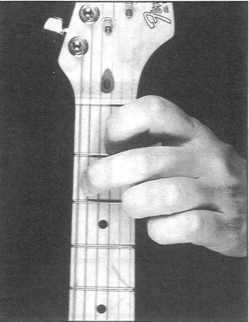

Key of A

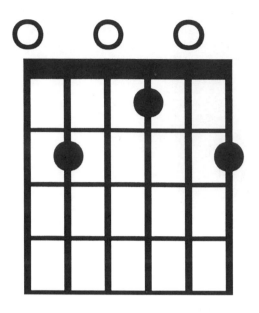

E9

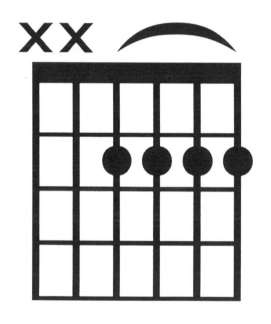

F#m7

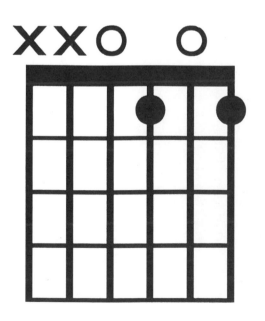

G#dim

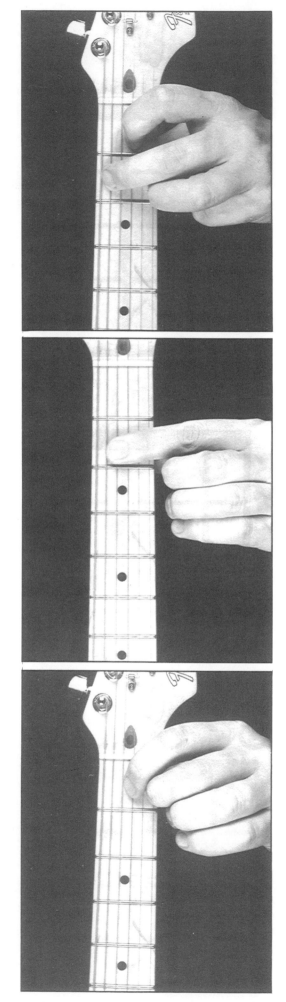

Key of B♭

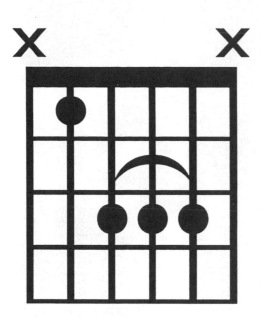

B♭

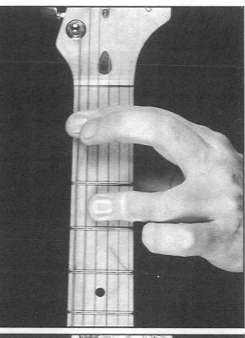

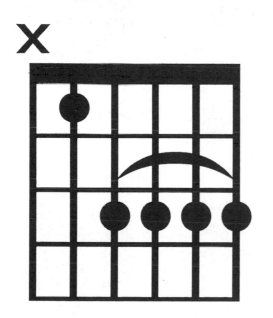

B♭6

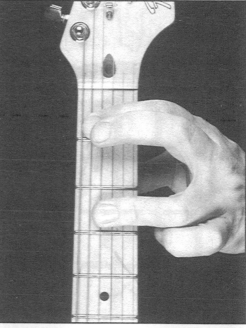

B♭maj7

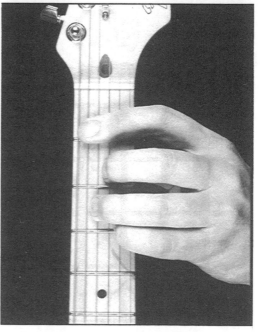

Key of B♭

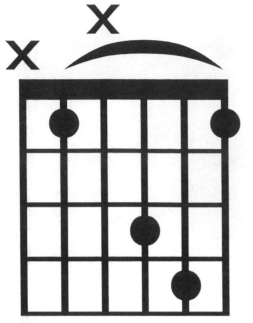

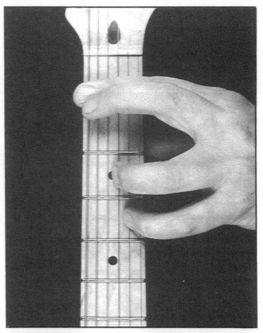

B♭ sus 4

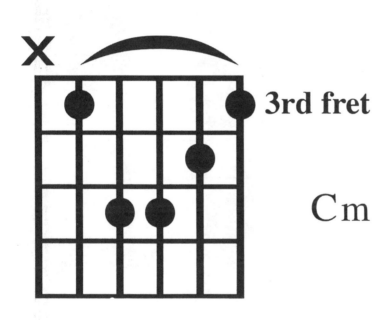

3rd fret

Cm

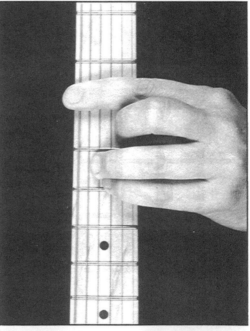

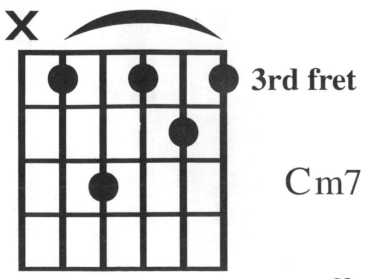

3rd fret

Cm7

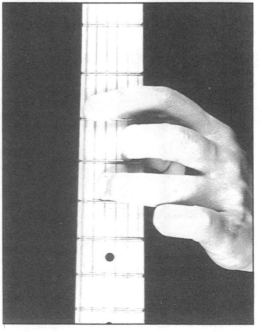

38

Key of B♭

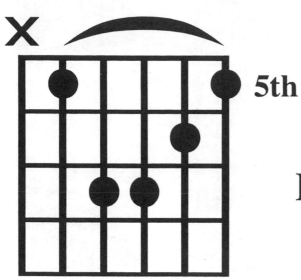

X

5th fret

Dm

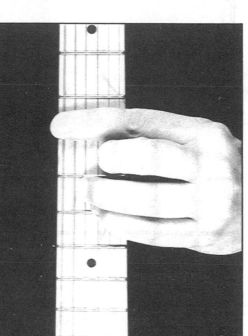

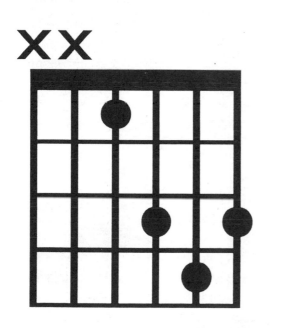

X X

E♭

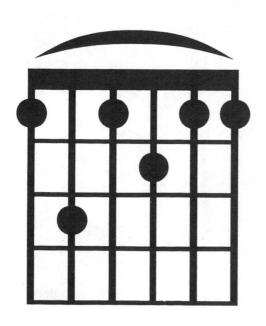

F7

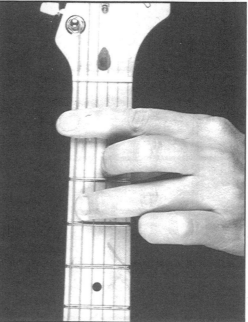

Key of B♭

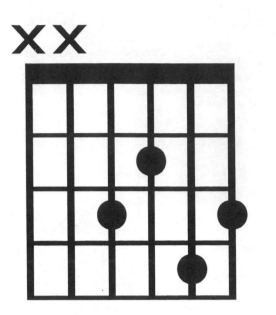

F9

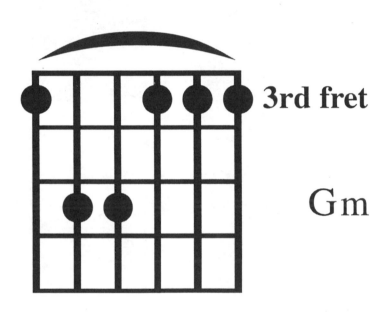

3rd fret

Gm

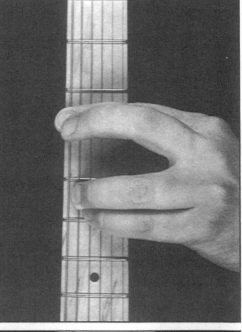

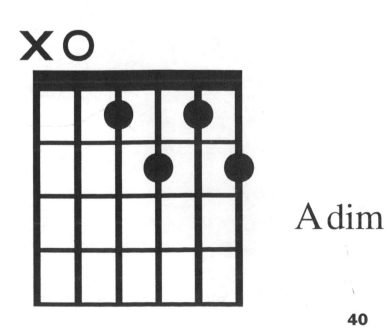

A dim

40